ARIES H(

Lisa Lazuli

This is a book of monthly horoscopes for 2018; due to request you can access daily horoscopes at:

http://dailyfreehoroscopes.siterubix.com/

Check out my youtube channel for political and world predictions and relationship astrology:

Lisa Lazuli Astrology

Contents

ARIES HOROSCOPE 2018

YEARLY OVERVIEW

This is a fierce year!

Aries are not a ballistic missile; this year, you, are a cruise missile, powerful, guided, and targeted. You are also a MOAB; ready to make a major impression and impose yourself on a situation to ensure you prevail.

While Aries are often good at initiating, you guys are not always great at keeping the momentum going and ramming home an advantage, but in 2018, you are able to keep that speed up, keep jumping over the hurdles and making sure you build on efforts and ensure that projects grow and develop.

You are quite formidable and will be a force to be reckoned with – anyone who underestimates you does so at their peril.

Aries will be influenced by the wider social order and yet you will also have your opportunity to change the world around you and have an impact and influence beyond your immediate circles.

They say with great opportunity comes great responsibility, and Aries will feel that pressure to perform and to carry not only their own dreams but the hopes and dreams of your family and even your community on your shoulders.

Often your progress is blocked by something which is mysterious and hard to put your finger on. Some of the problems you confront will not be able to be tackled logically or with the analysis of facts – you will have to use your gut feel and your ability to sense the motivations and deeper desires of those around you.

Much of what is important this year happens in the deep recesses of the mind – your subconscious and the subconscious of others, and so the more you understand and can use psychology, the better equipped you are to meet the challenges head on. Life is very much like a masked ball where the pretty, colourful masks can distract you from the machinations that are really under way at the party – it really isn't a party at all – it may be a murder mystery weekend.

Intrigue marks 2018, and Aries are not quite so comfortable with this – you are used to being out there – what you see is what you get, and you are loud and proud of that. The ram has a lot to learn from the Scorpion regarding being more cynical and crafty in the unorthodox and cunning way they set about tracking their prey. Aries need to be calculated and strategic about the way you formulate plans and somewhat ruthless in the way you attack. When I say ruthless, I do not mean heartless; being ruthless is all about knowing who your friends are and knowing who has your back and thereby knowing when you are going for the kill and where the knives will fall.

2018 is the year of 1000 knives for Aries who will cull many areas of life to make way for new people, new opportunities, and also new attitudes.

The need to reform is strong, and so if ever there is a year when you can go cold turkey (regarding a habit), adopt a strict and disciplined dietary routine or train for something gruelling, then this is it. Aries who have difficulties concerning health or who are undergoing rehabilitation can have remarkable success as you have an immense amount of spiritual energy which can be applied to goals involving physical or mental improvement and renewal.

Aries should tackle tough problems in 2018 – whatever you have avoided or allowed to go unchecked can now be put on the autopsy table, examined, analysed and then discarded for good.

Important goals, and I am not talking lofty goals or aspirational goals like travel or bucket lists, I mean life and death type goals which shape and define you as a person can be taken on with the help of the universe in getting resolution and progress.

Aries are quite conservative in 2018, and you will take a tough line on things, especially where there is a lack of respect for the law or rules and regulation. Even if you are generally liberal, in 2018, you can be far less tolerant, and you can develop stricter codes of what you believe you will and will not accept.

Aries can take a great deal of hardship without quitting; you can also suffer unfairness without getting defeatist. In fact, adversity drives you harder – now that is the Aries spirit, no sulking near the cookie jar like a depressed Taurus.

Rams are stoic in 2018, and you can put up with your stuffy selfish boss or with the pathetic regimented rules at the office as long as you know your plan is underway, and temporary submission is for a discernible long run cause.

Bone health is important, and so Aries need to make sure they get enough calcium, magnesium, and Vitamin D. Regarding dental health, co-enzyme q10 is essential. Avoid toffee, caramel popcorn, sugary drinks, and anything you know your dentist does not approve of as teeth are a sensitive area this year.

Aries need to be present this year – you must be aware of danger, and this can often be danger caused by your own obsession or tendency to get carried away. You almost need to be your own guardian angel, watching over yourself and seeing things as if from above and then asking yourself, why? Is there a good enough reason.

Sometimes this year you can be motivated by vengeance and a desire to get even; wrongs are not forgotten, and wounds are felt deeply. The key when you have these feelings is being able to put your ego on the shelf while your head takes care of the situation more dispassionately.

While you have great courage and also the nerve to hold it together when things are really tough and tense, you can be a little do or die where you make sacrifices which seem like great ideas at the moment, but which on reflection were not worth the outcome. Cut the extremes off your emotional chart and operate to the middle.

Willpower is highly developed and focused especially on matters of business, management, construction, money, and imposing or increasing your power and influence in any situation. Material or monetary gain could be significant this year, and money and power are allied in terms of your goals.

You have a high sex drive this year and yet to experience the best sex you may have to confront some deep seated insecurities and hang ups, often porn and experimentation can be sticking plasters for not dealing with psycho sexual issues. Sometimes, solving a sexual problem could throw light on wider psychological issues and can help you in other walks of life.

Aries are very sensual regarding love and more able to express yourself in an amorous and patient way; your stamina is improved, and you will spend more time to get what you want from love. While the air signs are the ones that may get you randy, it is the earth signs that can really do it for you in the sack, and so get ready to apologise to your Virgo friend who you said was boring, or else there will be no benefits for you.

With Mercury retrograde in your return chart, your thinking processes are generally more acute and incisive, and you may grasp concepts of nuance that others miss in their haste to see the obvious. Aries humour is dry and rather quirky, and you will enjoy a chuckle to yourself as you are prone to see the funny side of many situations.

You may be slower to take in new information – perhaps you are sceptical or unsure of its usefulness, and you will probably be unwilling to throw out what is tried and tested just to jump on some new bandwagon.

Aries are in many ways a doubting Thomas this year, with heightened cynicism and desire to research and delve deeper. At times, you may struggle with doubts and wonder why you do not see things as others do or are slower to accept them; you need to trust your inner wisdom and side step the folly of the masses.

While Aries are known to be quick fire speakers never shy of blurting out an opinion or a verbal dart, this year you are more likely to put your tongue in the holster on safe mode before you cock the verbal gun and fire.

Aries are very self-reliant; it is not that you do not trust others to get the job done – you just want to avoid disappointment and almost pre-empt a situation where you may be let down or have your illusions quashed.

You are very self-aware and more wary of setting yourself up for situations where you may fail or get egg on your face – Aries usually rush in where angels fear to tread and take the good with the bad, feeling that all is well that ends well; however, in 2018, you will need more certainty before you stick your neck out, and this only help you to be more effective and successful.

You are concerned about what others think of you; not that this will stop you being yourself and striking out in your typical Aries way, it will just ensure that when you strike out, you are that little bit more certain of a positive outcome and not gambling just so that you can be first.

In love, too much reason can be a barrier to understanding, and Aries need to pause to pick up the subtle and nonverbal forms of communication – deeds not words can tell you more about the relationships. In marriage and long-term relationships, it is vital to accept the quirks and the ups and down rather than trying to get out some emotional steam iron and flatten out all the creases for a perfect finish – the beauty of the relationship is in the flaws.

Problems in love should be tackled day to day and not micro analysed and dissected. This year, things will change fast in love, and so what is a problem today need not be one tomorrow and so keep rolling with the punches and do not linger on yesterday's argument or issue; it's gone like the rain of yesterday, and today is sunny so make hay.

Planning in relationships and looking for love to follow some standardised pattern is NOT the way to go in 2018. Many new relationships that start will be highly spontaneous in nature and will defy conventions in many ways. Love will follow an unconventional path but one that also has more excitement due to the unpredictability.

In sex, you cannot stick to a Friday Night Fish and Chips, then sex regime – it's about doing it whenever and wherever. Shake up your sex life with new toys, sex games, doing it at different times of the day and in different places. Throw out your rule book about sex and also relationships and embrace the chaos and confusion.

Regimented and controlling relationships that limit your emotional freedom and also stamp out self-expression will have to go. Indeed, Aries who have hankered and pined for love lost will find that there are far more colourful and exciting fish in the sea. In seeking new love, cast the net far and wide and embrace those who challenge you and your perception of life. Love this year is about embracing changes, thinking more liberally, and letting your hair down.

Your private life could well be injected with some surprising circumstances that jolt you out of unconscious yet pervasive thinking patterns and habit. In fact, limiting habits have to go this year – they are safety blankets, comfort zones that you really do not need. Look out for coincidences, especially if they make no sense – what is the universe trying to tell you and are you taking notice?

Aries may play the role of guardian angel to another, helping someone out behind the scenes, anonymously or via a cyber connection. You may develop a powerful relationship (not necessarily romantic) with a person you only ever meet online and never in person.

A secret you have kept for many years may suddenly come out, or you may become willing to talk about it and thus release yourself from the hold it has on you. Changes in your life may mean accepting that what was once private and off limit is now fair game, and it can be rather liberating once you accept this – in fact, it may open up your life in ways unimagined. By accepting things about yourself and being more open about your past, your vices and your suppressed desires, you can widen you social circle, your support network, and your contacts base, widening your points of reference and your whole world.

Career and money are big parts of this year with great progress possible regarding both. This can be a year of promotions and career advancement and also a substantial improvement in finances. In career, it is one of those 10 year overnight success cases when to all and sundry you look like you have nailed a plum job, but they do not know the work behind it. Often success that comes now was seeded many moons ago, and you have worked quietly away for it. Karma has much to do with your achievements now, and good work done ricochets back in positive ways; however, any corners cut in haste or false expectations are dashed. While you will achieve success this year, it may not be in the bag totally, and there may be a parole period of further proving yourself and showing you can handle the heat in the kitchen. Men and male mentor figures can play an important role, but their advice can also be harsh and hard to take at times – you cannot rest on laurels as you must keep learning and keep the pressure on.

Money comes to you often from others – you may find it easier to get funding or source funds for career development. Loan applications are often successful and for larger amounts and better terms than you thought; you must not extend more than you need to, however. Tax refunds, insurance pay outs, and even an inheritance or donation are possible. You can use the power and law of attraction to bring more money to you, but money tends to flow more when your need for it is motivated out of a desire for self-improvement, freedom, and personal development than material goals. Those who work in industries where you gain from tips or may receive gifts or kickbacks from clients can do very well – watch out for tax implications.

Father issues can rear their head, and it may be possible to develop a better relationship with a father who was absent or with whom you have always clashed. You may see your father in a new light in view of changed circumstances, and your changed attitude to him (even if the relationship is still hard work) can change your view of yourself and your role as a father/mother or parent and your future.

LIFE

The start of the year represents a very good time for Aries as you have a great deal of power courtesy of Jupiter and Pluto, the fuel injected planets, sure to propel you forward with pace helping you to make creative changes and to remake your immediate future and also your long-term future. You have a great deal of energy to effect the changes that can lead to goals being achieved and new ventures being set up.

Aries are known for always throwing themselves full throttle into activities, and you have a great deal of drive; what you often lack, however, is focus and also a long-term strategy. You tend to take aim and fire without really thinking what is next; however, right now you can sharpen that focus, pay more attention to the overall objective, and thus be much more effective at not only getting the job done but at prioritising and making your effects more effective in the long run.

This is a very purposeful period where you can feel as if the universe is on your side and wants you to do well; you can kick obstacles out of the way in your rambunctious style and shout, "Take that!"

Power comes your way quite easily, but take note, the universe is watching you and will observe how you use that power – if you use it to enhance your own needs while also benefitting those who collectively work with you or rely on you, then you can have added success. That is why this period is especially successful for those whose work is political and social spheres where your actions have far wider consequences.

You are competitive and ready to take on opposition head on.

HEALTH

This month is excellent for physical rehabilitation, and so if you are recovering from an accident or injury and having to undergo physio or do special exercises, then the force of the planets will help in your resilience and ability to stick with the regimes and benefit from them.

Your spiritual strength brings a boost to the physical as your faith in both yourself and your ability to improve health and fitness is strong. Positive thoughts mixed with solid exercise and fitness schedules can have remarkable results. You can have tremendous focus and determination in achieving sporting goals.

One negative is that you prefer to front run; coming from behind is not your favourite way, but you can still manage it.

A significant event this month could bring about an understanding of the deeper purpose of your life – in fact, a sense of underlying purpose is a key motivational factor for Aries. If you do not have a strong sense of purpose, you will seek it – often in weird and wonderful places.

LOVE

A very passionate and intense month where full blown love affairs can arise out of nothing. Hate is very close to love – something worth remembering. The one you love can bring out the very best and very worst in you, and passions are often inflamed. Conflict situations should be avoided, and when the volcanic lavas of anger rise, it is better to walk away.

Some time spent apart from you marriage partner can only be a good thing as with the heightened intensity, things can be like a pressure cooker and can spiral either up or down, and so you need that distance to see a perspective.

New relationships may have hidden motivations on one or both of your parts and Aries cannot be blind to this – you can also not hide from this or forget it. You must have your eyes wide open in love and not let the excitement draw you away from the potential dangers.

Aries are certainly daring in love, and not much will deter you from pursuing the one you have your eye on – you must be careful of fixation, and this is a year when romantic feelings are very intense and often take over the senses.

Loyalty is a massive issue this year, and this month, events will test that loyalty by throwing you both conundrums which can be very revealing of how far you will both go to defend or stand by each other.

Jealousy cannot be underestimated this month, and yet it is within your power to control the effects and the power it had over you – jealousy is one of the most powerful and destructive emotions, and it can cause havoc in relationships. However, Aries can use jealousy this month to transform their approach to the other in the relationships and also use it as a driver of self-awareness and understanding.

CAREER

Many of the changes that happen now happen quite spontaneously, and you can jump at the opportunity. This is a period where you need to spot the wave or the bandwagon and hop on board.

Much of what happens right now can work towards your ends even if at first it does not seem so, and so instead of being downhearted when odd circumstances thwart you, see it as a chance to reassess and perhaps spot a better way forward.

From the 16th of January onwards is a good time for starting new ventures, a new job or a new project. Up until the 16th is better for consolidation and finalising. The avenues of work favoured for expansion this month are loans and finance. After the 16th you may have success seeking loan extensions and additional finance for business. This will also be a good time for important decisions you make regarding financial advice you give others. Contracts with new business partners and also insurance claims and business structure changes should be made after the 16th.

This is a good month for any business restructuring or for selling a part of a business.

A very good month for new initiatives to promote your services or goods – placing a new ad in the newspaper or doing a social media blitz can be very effective at drumming up interest.

Aries who work in alternate fields may write a paper or write for a publication – journalists may be interested in your work, and you could be interviewed.

Aries may lead academic research or could be promoted to head teacher or lecturer. Those of you in education can gain more influence and also have greater autonomy to lead in your field. Students can become more vocal or join student unions.

This is a very good month to be decisive and to cut out some parts of your business or your ties to something completely. Kill off anything that has lingered and move on.

FEBRUARY 2018

LIFE

After the solar eclipse on the 15th of February, things take off again, and you can use the power of the lunar cycle to begin making plans, finalising agreements and starting new courses of action during the next 15 days. The first 15 days of Feb are better for completion and consolidation. What you should, however, avoid from Feb 15 are excursions involving the sea or ferries or getting tied up in the money or finances of friends. Avoid giving friends free advice, especially if you are a professional and if the advice will be used for family purposes. Contracts involving hospitals, care homes, social services, and other medical institutions may lose you money or have unexpected outcomes. The latter part of Feb is a great time for managerial decisions and putting yourself or your company into the limelight; it is also a good time to accept a position of power or greater responsibility. Creative work gets a boost as the month goes on, especially where Aries work with their hands to fashion products.

Aries who are taking some time off to do creative work can have a very successful and productive month as you experience a deep connection with what you do, and you will feel more tuned in to the collective unconscious from which you can draw inspiration. Aries are closer to the bone, more in tune with the vibe, and you have just that little extra intuitive power to draw meaning out of both everyday events and also wider social affairs.

Aries may be called to do some charitable or pro bono work; you may find yourself involved in some complex issue to do with your mother's extended family, and these may become quite tricky emotionally as nothing is what it seems.

HEALTH

Aries need to pay attention to health this month as you may be prone to infections and also allergic reactions – your best bet is to be consistent and to stick with what you know not trying any outlandish remedies or off the wall cures.

Support your immune system with extra Vitamin D and also Zinc and Vitamin C (the last two taken together preferably); you should also increase your intake of kale, broccoli, and cabbage.

While it is not like Aries to be depressed as you are highly proactive people who seek solutions, you may experience a dip mid-month where you cannot quite yet use the power of the solar eclipse to move forward as you are low in energy, motivation, or willpower. Your lack of motivation has much to do with an inner confusion that is making you wonder whether what you are doing is the right thing. During this phase, you cannot force the issue; you should sit back and allow the feelings to wash over you and thoughts to come to you rather than chasing down the solutions. Moments alone or doing a creative pursuit or even immersing yourself in charity work or something totally contrary to your ego drives can be strangely enlightening.

LOVE

"What is essential is invisible to the eye, only the heart can see rightly." Aries want to be like 007's martini when it comes to love, i.e., shaken and stirred. Even difficult and upsetting events in your love life can be fulfilling if they reveal depth of feeling and a multi-layered, multi-dimensional level of emotion. What Aries cannot stomach is shallowness, and you will walk right away from relationships where there are a facade and a front – you will also have scant patience with people who are uptight and unwilling to share.

New relationships can start in unusual circumstances, often where the Arian is playing Good Samaritan and doing a good deed.

Spiritual interests are often a uniting force in new relationships and can speed up the bonding even where you are very different and know very little about each other.

You sex drive is high, and you are also very romantic, and yet for a change, Aries are patient and willing to do the foreplay to make sure that the intimate moments are that much sweeter –the passion starts long before the bedroom, and much of the romance is in deeds and body language, what is unspoken but suggested is highly erotic.

Aries in long-term relationships where there is only a superficial connection can feel both lonely and also empty; if you cannot inject meaning into your relationship and revive the emotional connection, is it worth staying?

CAREER

Aries need to be careful of online security and also with passwords as even large and reputable companies could be subject to hacking, and your information could be lost. Make sure you tick the relevant box to avoid information sharing where possible. Make sure your information is backed up on laptops or computers that are totally offline. You should also take care to check your bank balance as if you do not keep up to date with daily changes you may not catch a security breach or cyber theft fast enough. You must also be alert to scams and hoaxes, especially after the middle of the month.

Sales and customer relations are improved come the end of the month, and you will get stronger and stronger results as the month goes on.

The solar eclipse on the 15th stimulates your idealistic nature and also your desire to work with others to pool talent and resources and achieve more. Together we are stronger is the theme, and Aries are a uniting and inspiring force who can bring together those with diverse ideas and opinions to act for a common purpose.

Improving your networks and learning how to use them more effectively is important – it is not enough to network (both in person, the old-fashioned way, and also online) if you do not know how to exploit those connections. Networks work both ways – give and receive and so make sure you offer encouragement and also a loud and vocal voice of optimism for those in your field.

It is important to be true to yourself and not to follow the crowd – be a torch bearer for both truth and champion ideas that take things forward not back.

Aries have vision right now, and a greater grasp of what your life could be, and so use this time to set some goals – not all goals have to be practical and achievable, you should have a fair few 'punts' in there as well, i.e., long shots which just, maybe just come off.

LIFE

It is vital to draw on past experience in order to further your aims, and the universe will test whether you have learned the lesson of the past, even the subtle ones.

Your energy is high this month, and you have creativity, ingenuity, and the ability to work with people. You can offer spontaneous leadership where required or just step into a new role and start doing it as if you were born for the position. You have a natural flair and confidence and can adapt quickly and make needed changes while keeping momentum going.

Aries love novelty, and you will want to be doing whatever is 'in' or 'cool'; you have an eye out for both fashion trends and also new directions and ideas in your fields of interest. You can embrace new ideas with courage, and a 'nothing ventured nothing gained' spirit of enterprise.

The best period for important decisions, meetings, and beginning new activities is between the 17th of March with the new Moon and the 23rd when Mercury goes retrograde. Activities begun prior to March 17 are during the waning moon, and thus may not have the longevity or the most prosperous outcome. After the 23rd Aries should avoid activities which involve important communications, i.e., press releases, publishing, and public speaking unless of course, you do these every day. In general, after the 23rd will be a period when communications will run less smoothly and be subject to confusions and interruptions. Short distance travel and logistical issues may also suffer setbacks and delays or frustrations. Decisions regarding property, procurement, your suppliers, children, friends, or politics can be made with success after the 17th.

HEALTH

This month will be physically active with greater emphasis on sports, and you will also have greater energy to expend in your social life. You can work hard and play hard; it is vital to balance mental work with physical exertion. Water sports and dance can be excellent ways to relax and get your endorphins going; Aries should avoid those sports which are hard on the joints.

Aries have immense determination this month, and so if you want to start a diet or a demanding training regime, this is the time.

Mercury which rules your 6th house of health is retrograde from the 23rd of the month, and so this is the period when you need to pay more attention to your health – listen to your body and attend to small aches, pains, or symptoms. You should use this time to think more about your health, especially when it comes to the amount of time you spend staring at a computer screen or sitting at a desk. Try and incorporate greater variety in both your diet and exercise regime as they may be lop sided, tending to cater for one part of your body and not another. Make sure you do stretches to increase flexibility.

The mind-body connection is also vital, and with Mercury retrograde square Pluto, you cannot ignore the psychological element of any health issue. Look deep and look below the surface for solutions to problems and get at the root cause, which as is indicated can be in mental issues or anxiety.

Time to tackle obsessive tendencies and also negative thought patterns like resentment and bitterness. Use this time to examine your thought patterns and attitudes and to adjust them to more positive ones.

You have a desire to push your own limits, and while you should take care not to go too far, you can make some achievements that will surprise you.

Surgical procedures can be very successful at this time.

LOVE

Aries are very intense and quite demanding this month, and so you may need to give your partner a bit of space and respect them if they want some breathing room as you can be hard to be with full time. Aries need sexual satisfaction, but you must not be lazy about the romance or the foreplay – no wham bam thank you, ma'am, you need to pay close attention at setting the scene and getting the vibe just right or you risk alienating your sexual partner.

Sudden sexual liaisons with friends are possible – Aries are easily turned on, and you may make a move on a long-term friend; this often does not work out, but it could well suit you both temporarily. Communication is vital; however, you need to be sure that the sex does not spoil the friendship, and asking the right questions can nip anything in the bud.

Aries have the ability to go direct to the heart of the matter and address what is really important – at times you can be blunt, and you may not steer clear of asking pertinent questions about personal matters.

Aries want to talk about sex, and you are willing to open up about what you want and even how you would like to experiment. Aries can enjoy sexual banter, and saucy exchanges over instant message or text can be very arousing. You can be a little impatient with partners who are coy and evasive. New relationships must offer some adventure and something a little exotic and daring; this is not a time where Aries go for the girl next door.

CAREER

After the 15th of March, Aries are ready to take action regarding finances and loans. This is a good time to deal with financing arrangement and make changes where possible. The latter stage of the month favours investigation and detailed analysis. Aries can make quite radical financial decisions right now and yet if they are in line with strategies and goals that matter, it can be quite appropriate.

This is a time to rebel against groups and be more daring with your ideas and initiatives – Aries are the ones to put forward more radical and far-reaching proposals. Aries will seek to break arrangements with any bodies or organisations which curtail your freedom or restrict you; this a period where you have to get rid of anything which confines your thoughts or gives you negative messages about what you can and cannot achieve. We are always told what we cannot do rather than what we can do – now you need to detach from any person or group that gives you these limiting and negative messages.

This month is good for intensive concentration and mental work, and yet Aries can find some of the detail required a little tedious; you need to push through with the boring side of work in order to get to what fulfils you.

Aries can be more critical and exacting and yet you have to focus on being more diplomatic when expressing these views as you can come across as a little cold and harsh in your appraisals. You see the truth and the bones of the matter, but your way of expressing this is not to everyone's taste as not everyone is ready for the truth, so go gently and call it as you see but gradually.

From the 15th Aries will have the chance to seize power and take more control over their destiny – use any twists of fate to your advantage, and do not hold back – when you sense a window of opportunity, grab it.

APRIL 2018

LIFE

With Chiron entering your first house, Aries have the power to make the best of what may seem to be a limiting or a bad situation. Often it is the struggles you face which define you more than your successes and which shape you and compel you to discover a talent you may otherwise never develop. So this month can be very exciting for those of you interested in the deeper meaning of life and the significance of the fights we face.

Failure is often fertile ground for success to grow in and so mistakes or hiccoughs must be seen as opportunities to learn, to learn fast and well, and to improve and refine. Mistakes you make now or have made in the past must be taken as lessons to improve rather than indications that you should stop pursuing a course. There is also a need for Aries to pass on lessons learned to others who may be at the juncture you once were, and if you can pass on the lessons, there is good karma within that.

March 31 to April 15 is the time of the waning moon, and new projects or important arrangements should be avoided where possible. From April 15, it is all systems go again, and so you can start putting your foot down.

HEALTH

This month will be physically active with greater emphasis on sports, and you will also have greater energy to expend in your social life. You can work hard and play hard; it is vital to balance mental work with physical exertion. Water sports and dance can be excellent ways to relax and get your endorphins going, Aries should avoid those sports which are hard on the joints.

Aries have immense determination this month, and so if you want to start a diet or a demanding training regime, this is the time.

You have a desire to push your own limits, and while you should take care not to go too far, you can make some achievements that will surprise you.

Surgical procedures can again be very successful at this time.

LOVE

Jupiter turning retrograde in your 8th house has some exciting and yet also explosive manifestations. When the expansive and enterprising planet Jupiter turns retrograde in the 8th all that energy goes underground and creates a pressure cooker environment. Aries need to manage their jealousy, possessiveness, and sexual desire carefully as it is hard to sweep things under the carpet – as if you do they tend to build up like a volcano; however, it is also not easy to be open with your partner as with Jupiter and Mercury both retrograde communicating and being open minded and tolerant is hard as emotions, especially the deep seated and explosive ones can get the better of you.

In new relationships, it may all be about sex, but the sex can be overpowering in its intensity and passion, so much so that everything else pales into insignificance and you enter your own bubble of excitement – this relationship can have compulsive and obsessive elements, not all of which are healthy.

Fetishes may be something which unite you and a new partner, and this is a period where certain sexual practices or fetishes bring more satisfaction and are great fun.

This period is one where it may not be easy to share and so not a good time for starting a joint bank account or arranging a pre nup, even in new relationships there can be issues around sharing expenses. Boundaries are very important and to avoid problems each of you has to respect the other's red lines.

It is a time of understanding the deeper psychological aspects that operate in the relationship and which drive many of the things you do or arguments you have – nothing can be resolved by looking at superficial day to day problems – you must unearth the key fears, insecurities, and desires that drive the more overt emotions.

CAREER

Mercury retrograde in your first house encourages Aries to press the pause button and also the reset button regarding the way you project yourself. You need to perhaps redo your CV or your Linked In profile, and if you regularly use the same speech or presentations, you need to bin that and start from scratch. This is not a time of rehashing old techniques or using the same words, you must modernise your output and pay attention to trends, modern vernacular, and humour.

If you have a paper or report to submit, give it another read – it could be better. Any words you communicate to the public are a reflection of you, and so you want it to be the best reflection of you and so no quick fixes or short cuts, be thorough and exhaustive.

With Mercury retrograde square Pluto, this month you need to look at matters deeply, analysing the facts, looking for more facts and being highly critical of any information which comes your way. Be more aware of the psychological issues at play; look for hidden motivations, and always take account of what is behind the mask of others you deal with.

Powerful and forceful changes can start bubbling up within your work life – as yet it can be hard to make out what the outcome will be, but you will become increasingly aware that the tide is turning, and soon many oppressive and limiting circumstances will pass away.

This is a month when you need to be careful of how and what you spend – outlays may not have the effect you wish for. Loan extensions, other borrowings and also accepting investment from a silent partner or relative should be undertaken with caution or delayed. If you receive tips, gifts, company car or bonuses, be careful of the tax implications as these may cost more than they are worth.

Be careful of expert opinions or the advice of accountants or lawyers, etc. – make sure they have full information as their advice or calculations may be compromised as they do not have the full facts – make sure you review any information you pay for or commission which is passed onto you to see how accurate or sensible it is.

LIFE

Your optimism and your enthusiasm are high, but you are not very self-aware, and that can mean you misjudge certain situations – this is not the best time to put yourself on the line with an important judgment call, and you should hold back on making very strident opinions known as you may set yourself into a corner which is hard to climb down from.

Aries crave recognition, and you want to push yourself forward into situations where you think you are going to make an impression, but things are unlikely to turn out as you wish, especially if you act out of character or in a way which is in contrast to your usual persona. If you want to grab the headlines in your sphere of influence, you must capitalise on your position or build on what you have rather than striking out in on unrelated tangent.

Cheerfulness and a certain amount of luck can help you avoid the problems you will create while leaping before you look.

Aries are likely to clash with institutions this month – your own attitudes are likely to be at odds with prevailing rules and regulations being pushed down your throat, and you are never one to take things lying down.

Post-May 15 is great for starting any action or making decisions on almost any matter; however, the best results will come from deliberate action on bucket lists, applying for patents, finalising scientific projects, new IT initiatives, mass communications, and networking.

HEALTH

While health is rather good this month and Aries have a strong spirit within which keeps your mood high and your body's power to regenerate and recuperate strong, you have to ensure that ventures you get involved in to do not get out of hand, due to lack of planning and forethought and end up taking too much time or energy. Know your limits; you are attracted to adventure and outdoor activities, and these can benefit you as long as you do not dive right in thinking it's a doddle when there really is more to it.

Make sure you do not overburden yourself with responsibility just because you need to prove yourself. Stop seeking assurance in the wrong places and look to cultivate self-approval and self-acceptance internally.

LOVE

Love can be confused with a more general mood which has gripped you. Aries may fall in love fast this month, but often you are in love with an idealised version of that person, or you may be in love with them as they are reinforcing your opinions and beliefs. Love is also strongly linked to the activities you are immersed in, and so love relationships may develop with colleagues or associates who you are working closely with, but will these relationships last when the task is done, or the phase is over? It may be a love born of highly specific circumstances rather than an attraction based on your true selves.

Secret romances are possible this month as Aries are liable to be involved in liaisons which are unorthodox or unusual and which carry a deep meaning and engender a powerful emotional reaction within you.

Marriages can either be a bubble of enjoyment which helps you escape the hard realities of the world or a sphere of life where you feel disappointed and lonely. In either case, the choice is with you; it is all down to your underlying emotional outlook rather than what is really happening. Right now, illusions feel more real than what is real, and so to change reality you must change your outlook or detach yourself until your mood levels out, and you are more practical in outlook. Often past relationships cast a long shadow, and it can be hard to judge matters right now on their own merits as you keep relating things to the past and almost creating self-fulfilling prophecies.

This is quite a spontaneous month for Aries, and you will throw caution to the wind – you may embark on highly combustible relationships which only last a few days but which you are OK to bin once the excitement goes out.

Relationships with fixed signs and the earth signs suffer the most challenges for Aries or should I say that you can be very challenging for them to deal with as you are so unpredictable, highly strung, and lively. Only dynamic relationships and those which allow freedom, total self-expression, and are not judgemental can thrive this month.

CAREER

Aries are highly susceptible to the spiritual realm at this time, and I know that many Arians work as psychics, healers, alternative therapists, etc., and you have added power to tap into universal energies in order to bring greater understanding of your clients and get better results. If you are still learning or training in these fields, you can gain confidence.

This month is a very moving time for Aries involved in group activities or movements – you are fond of any activity where you gather en masse with others with some great idea or ideal to espouse. While Aries are natural leaders, right now you want to lose yourself in a sea of emotion or to be swept along in a tide of powerful or purposeful anger – you have to draw a line when this feeling becomes hysterical.

Aries must be more discriminating as you are not always selective enough about who you throw your hat in with – often carried away in the moment, associations look good, but when the hype dies down, you may feel you have been pulled in the wrong direction.

This is an ideas rich phase but not necessarily a practical one – it is great for brainstorming and allowing your imagination free reign, but you may have to delegate out the more logical details or leave them for another day.

This is good month to initiate activities which require joint action and cooperation.

Creatively, you have to make some sacrifices as not all the ideas or plans can come to pass as they cannot co-exist due to restrictions on resources – Aries must wield the axe and decide what course of action has the most chance of success and must have your full attention.

LIFE

This is a very good month for targets and for pinning yourself down to a routine. Yes, I now Aries can be allergic to routines, and you hate being boxed in and having to knuckle down to boring stuff that involves the kind of work only Taurus and Capricorn should even have to face; however, great progress and achievement can come from applied mental efforts this month. Diligence is repaid as is attention to detail and ironing out of the facts and figures.

Aries must get down to the nitty-gritty of any situation and sink your teeth into it – you may need to be very critical, and often you have to be ruthless regarding canning ideas or courses of action that are not cutting the mustard.

Sometime this month Aries' words may seem critical and harsh, but you have little truck with niceties, and you feel the need to be highly pragmatic, and that means dealing with the stuff others have swept under the carpet or have refused to acknowledge.

It is easier than usual for you to make quick and yet hard decisions. While Aries always prefer to deal directly, this is even more important this month and so pick up to phone and have a one to one or say it to someone's face, as although it may be uncomfortable, they will respect you more in the long run.

While you are serious and committed to goals and decisions, you are also enthusiastic and not about to let that big picture totally fade into the distance while you grapple with minutia.

Aries' desire to solve problems is strong, and you are resolute, your mental energy levels high, and along with a proactive and logical mind, you can conquer most problems mentally.

Aries are giving Capricorn a run for their money this month; you will be stealing their crown for being the most dogged and hard working.

HEALTH

You may be spending a lot of time on your feet and walking, and so you need to have a good and comfortable pair of shoes, not a time to be vain about footwear – better safe than sorry. Ankles, calves, and lower legs in general are vulnerable to injury and strain, and so take care when playing squash or sports where you have to change direction quickly and where there is pressure on lower joints. Use strapping or do lower impact exercise.

Aries need to eat plenty of eggs and also oily fish this month. You can also take Vitamin B complex, omega oil supplements and iron-rich foods like spinach and legumes.

Getting enough sleep is vital, and you need to know when enough is enough and it is time to can the work for the day.

LOVE

Aries can be a little emotionally frustrated this month – your feelings are running very high, and you are keen to enjoy love and relationships, and yet events are not always in your favour, and you are not that good at expressing what you want in a way that makes getting it possible. Timing seems to be working against you; you may just be about to cuddle up with your partner after a nice chat and a soothing glass of something grape related when you hear, "Mommy, I can't sleep," and your evening of sexual entertainment is gate-crashed.

But Aries, have you forgotten how good you are at management in other areas of your life? Maybe your private life needs some more planning and organising to ensure you get some affection and excitement. I know Aries want love to be spontaneous and planning somewhat dampens the fun, but plan free time within which you can be spontaneous.

In new relationships, Aries are beginning to wonder whether their new date is suitable – it could be that you are sexually incompatible or while there is chemistry, the actual modes and means you both enjoy just do not match up. It may also be that some of your new partner's opinions and habits are quite opposed to you and grate on you, even anger you. If you are a person who likes an 'opposites attract' style relationship, which Aries often do, this can work for the time being, but you will already be thinking there is a sell by date fast approaching.

Aries are awash with powerful desires, and they are not all about sex; they can also be about goals you want to set for the relationships, and you wish your partner would share your enthusiasm, which may not always be the case. You can clash about priorities and money, and often you will be sitting at opposite ends of the couch after starting a fairly innocuous conversation.

But amorous feelings are stimulated now, and they can often win the day with fights turning into great sex – intense and heartfelt communications even if angry turn you on.

In dating situations, Aries have to be more attuned to subtle signals, and you must pick up on the mood, or you could come on too strong or too eager. Strive for a balance between taking the initiative and being sensitive and aware of others' needs and wants. If you are however shy, this month, a boost in confidence can help you break out of your romantic shell and get back in the dating game again.

Relationships that are all about sex rather than love and compatibility can actually thrive this month; new relationships which begin can be just about good sex and not much else as you may have little in common and not very much to talk about, but you just drive each other wild and enjoy the sex. These relationships can be with Leo or Sagittarius or even Scorpio.

If your partner wants to please you, they must give you attention as one thing Aries cannot stand this month is aloofness and detachment – if you partner is cold and unresponsive, you will go looking for sports or social activities away from the relationship. You want your love like vindaloo not chicken salad this month.

CAREER

Uranus entering your 2nd house this month signifies the start of a lengthy period that cannot be ignored regarding your finances. Aries will be encouraged to develop more flexibility in the way you work and earn money. They say that today's workers under 40 will have up to five careers in their lifetime as the pace of change and also the impact of AI is getting faster and faster. Aries need to be hyper vigilant about change in their industry and look to either take advantage or get out before the change engulfs you. This is an exciting prospect for Aries who enjoy having a dynamic life and are never shy of a new challenge.

Social media marketing and using communication tools where you bypass traditional media to promote yourself or sell your products will become more and more of a tool you find yourself using. Aries looking for new careers must consider IT, hacking, cyber security, protection of intellectual property, and also online publishing as options. Look to learn new techniques but also look to be an innovator in your field. This is a very inventive time when Aries can find new ingenious solutions by your own efforts to solve often individual problems.

Independence becomes a massive issue for Aries now, and financial independence is a large part of that, and so for any of you who have been under the control of someone or something because you lacked finances, you can look forward to having more say in your destiny and more flexibility with finances.

Job share arrangements, scientific apprenticeships, flexi time, and working from home and other non 9-5 arrangements are possibilities on the horizon, and this is the start of a very liberating and successful time for Aries who want to combine motherhood with work.

Uranus' entry into Taurus signifies a seven year period where the finances of Aries get an overhaul, a revolution, and a boost. The changes you have made in terms of your own personal approach, making opportunities and entering new phases now begins to have its impact on your finances, so you are reaping rewards of changes you have made, and if you have not made changes in the obvious parts of your life, your finances may not be the arena of life where change comes to you.

LIFE

This month brings energy which is perfect for Aries who are in a
state of flux in their lives – "You say yes, I say no.
You say stop, and I say go go go, oh no."

Often on a new path or in-between paths, you wonder if you are
doing the right thing and the universe is giving you a big YES and
encouraging you to up the speed, ring the changes, and get fully
behind a new course of action. Daring and groundbreaking, Aries
can come into their element; there are opportunities for you to excel
as events will demand the decisive and bold moves Aries are so good
at.

You need to rally others around you as you may need more
cooperation than you think at the outset – be careful who you
alienate, try and keep people on side and act inclusively. Be a
unifying force and offer others the chance to prove to you what they
can do without dismissing them out of hand.

Aries are eager for adventure this month, and that can mean a variety
of things other than skydiving or hanging off a cliff face; some of the
best adventures you can have right now are being in situations which
challenge you or take you out of a comfort zone, handling it despite
reservations and learning something new about yourself that
surprises you. Often the most worthwhile surprises in life are those
little things which life teaches us about ourselves; things we might
never have known if we had not maybe pushed the boat out and had
a go or exposed ourselves to a new idea.

Positive action leads to positive results, and even if the outcomes are
very different to what you expected, they can still be highly
fortuitous.

Nothing happens by luck right now; you make your own luck by attempting, by trying and by pushing at one of your boundaries – embrace and tackle fears and limits.

July 12 to July 26 is the best time to begin new projects, start businesses, and ventures, and take risks.

HEALTH

With Jupiter at Quincunx your sun, but going direct you have to watch out for impulsive actions like eating, drinking too much, and also spending too much. You are not in a mood for holding back, and you will go with whatever seems like a good idea at the time. You quickly become caught up in the party mood, and you are not one to hang back like a wet blanket and say no.

Probably the best advice is to enjoy yourself but keep the Rennies, the Pepto-Bismol, and any other stomach soothers handy for the aftermath.

This month is great for team sports and activities as you feel more motivated when acting in tandem with others even though your competitive side still wants the team to follow your rules.

LOVE

Hidden agendas in love are something Aries often overlook naively, and yet any new relationship may have plenty of these, and so you should be more cautious and perhaps less open – do not give a new romantic partner a window into your soul, letting them have a peek at your vulnerabilities so they can hone in on them. Aries' naiveté in love is often a saving grace as perhaps if you were more aware, you would get drawn into things which really are not becoming of a forthright, honest Arian; however, not having that intuition firing can mean you get way too far down that garden path and waste valuable time.

This is not the best month for making financial arrangements with a partner, and you may clash over money – money arguments can reveal control issues which you need to take note of and not ignore.

Probably not the best month to start a sexual relationship, although having said that, with passion in the world of Aries running so high, I am sure it is a risk you want to take.

If single, Aries need to take a long hard look at what they want from a relationship – indeed, even if you are dating, ask yourself if you have settled for something that is below par. Why settle for second best? Is it down to fear, or perhaps you are paying too much attention to your age or to what stage of relationship your friends are at, or it may even be parental expectations. Time to evaluate what psychological drivers keep you in a place where you are unhappy and if these factors are rational. So make a list of your priorities in a relationship and see where the current one ranks – there is a whole world out there, Aries, and you love adventure so get out there and crack the case romantically.

CAREER

You are on a mission, and you want to have others on that ship sailing into the sunset with you; do not reject help or advice, take it on board whether you end up using it or not.

Financially, things are moving again this month, and any problem with financing or loans for your business project can clear up giving you greater flexibility and scope. While financially things get rolling again, this is not a good month to take on more debt or apply for additional financing over and above what you already have. You should try and cut your pattern according to your cloth and make cuts rather than extending overdrafts. Aries must also be careful of the fine print in current arrangements as things may be more complex than you first imagined, and there may be knock-on implications for tax.

Aries can count on support from more experienced or authority figures who can offer advice or practical support – you should make sure that money offered does not come with strings attached. Renewing ties to old student friends or colleagues from your early days on the career ladder are possible and could be solidified into productive working relationships.

This is a very resourceful month when you make the most of what you have in terms of resources and also manpower and skills. You have enough energy for new money-making projects and for stepping up existing ones. One pitfall is taking risks just to prove yourself – be secure in yourself and do not push yourself on another's behalf; only takes risks which will make you feel good about yourself.

There may be conflicts over issues of ownership, and so make sure you are clear on your rights and obligations in any hire purchase arrangement or deal where you are pooling money or sharing a bit of equipment. Make sure physical stock and goods are insured against fire.

LIFE

With Mercury retrograde in the 5th house, this can be a tricky month in dealing with children and also making decisions about them; you may keep changing your mind and questioning whether you are doing the right thing or not. Advice from others or from websites can be even more confusing. Worry about children can also make you edgy, and you have less confidence in your abilities as a parent – on the positive side, you will be searching for more information and taking much more time over any decision you make, and that can only be a good thing. When you look back over the month, you will realise that amid what felt like dilemmas and impossible choices, much was learned, and your communication skills with your children improved.

Mercury goes direct again on the 19th of August marking the beginning of more clarity and the green light for decision making regarding children and also your creative projects.

The end of the month is good for large scale parties and celebrations and can also be a very busy time for those of you involved in the entertainment business, especially crime writers, dramatists, and those in alternative music.

The solar eclipse on the 11th of August is a perfect excuse to find a party to go to, arrange a spontaneous do, or to hell with it, strip down and turn up the stereo while you vacuum as no matter what the weather climatically, the universe says it is a fine, fine time to party today and during the coming weeks. Use any excuse to be young again and indulge in activities that make you feel young and vibrant.

Anything you do for enjoyment will seem twice as good right now, almost as if it has extra sugar and a coating of chocolate sprinkles.

Self-consciousness and concern about what 'they' think are more easily cast off as you embrace life and the joy of it.

HEALTH

Is the work you are putting into your career furthering long-term aims, or is it just a means to a monthly end? Could the effort you put into your work be more productively aimed regarding enhancing long-term prospects instead of just being a pay cheque. What sacrifices do you make for the sake of work, and which are worth it? Family matters may force you to revaluate goals this month.

Aries are highly impatient and impetuous in the first half of the month, and you can be quite reckless as you are impatient with any limitation or restriction which slows you down – make sure you read instructions, listen properly, and follow speed limits to avoid injury. While you may enjoy theme parks, adventure sports, and other thrilling experiences this August, make sure you do them safely. Mars in Capricorn square Uranus in Taurus can mean injuries to the bones or whiplash.

LOVE

With Mercury retrograde in the 5th house until the 19th; romantic matters can be subject to a state of flux, and it can be hard to know whether you are coming or going. Romantic encounters can spring out of thin air, offering much with great conversation, banter, and a seemingly effervescent fizz, and all of a sudden they fizzle right out, and you may be left wondering what the hell was going on. Ghosting can be a problem, and so watch out for ghosters who come on strong and then disappear into thin air as if they were a cube of ice that evaporated into a hot August night.

With Mars in square retrograde to Uranus also retrograde, Aries have to be careful that they are also not guilty of ghosting too. Your enthusiasms flare up almost as if you are subject to an electricity surge, and while in the state of heightened awareness and almost electric energy you tend to be very gung-ho, but you also get bored fast and that can influence feelings in love which can change quickly leaving the other person spinning like a top.

In marriages, this month can be harder if you are at home and working to a routine as you are supercharged and dull chores and admin tasks will hardly inspire – you may be more irritable or irrationally angry unless you can find new challenges from DIY, to garden landscaping to revamping your home. Challenges should improve your day to day lifestyle. Taking up new sports or throwing yourself into a socially inspiring project can also alleviate the pressure on relationships. If you are on holiday, this is far more manageable as you can indulge yourself with your partner in fun and energetic activities which at least quench your desire for novelty and stimulation.

Affairs are a possibility as you are rebellious and will throw caution to the wind,

but you should not think that these will no leave destruction in their wake regarding home and family. Actions now have consequence down the line, not immediately.

CAREER

The total lunar eclipse of July 27 will impart effects into the month of August. For Aries, the lunar eclipse is in your 11th house of hopes, dreams, and the collective. This says to me many Aries will reach either a culmination or a tipping point regarding career. It could be that you have achieved what you want to in a position and have nothing else to give that particular job and you need to move on, or it could mean that you reach a turning point internally where you know that your future lies elsewhere and after the August break or at the end of summer you have to make the break and try something new. As there is this link to the 5th house of self-expression and also children, family considerations are paramount to the decisions you reach about career – work-life balance, childcare, overall priorities and your fundamental happiness can no longer be ignored. The eclipse may not come alongside any final decision, but it can be the time when inside yourself you sense a change, and you realise there is no going back.

From the 19th when Mercury goes direct, and the moon is waxing, Aries can once again hit the accelerator especially regarding your creative projects and problem-solving initiatives. This is a time when you can more effectively put your stamp on any activity you are involved in by presenting and tackling it in a positive individualistic way. This is a period where style matters more than substance, and while you should always make sure what you do has value and is full of merit at the core, this month you cannot neglect the package your message comes in – PR, marketing, presentation, and entertainment value matter, so make sure your content stands out.

The end of the month is an important one for investments, gains can be made with stocks and shares, but close attention must be paid to longer term trends in your analysis to make the most of the opportunities. Options, i.e. shorts and puts can be profitable.

The solar eclipse in Leo gives a boost to any creative project, and you'll find that your juices flow faster and more freely than usual.

In all ventures, there can be a fine line between playful adventure and risky thrill-seeking behaviour, so try to tread that fine line.

LIFE

September 9 is the new moon, and it waxes until September 24, making the intervening period the best time for events, decisions, and important dates and arrangements. The sun in positive aspect to Jupiter and Pluto means that decisions regarding money, insurance, and finances are favoured. It is also a good time to seek tax advice and use an investment analyst. Any group counselling, psychotherapy, and sex or relationship counselling proceeds productively between these dates.

Aries do have to be a little careful of whose influence you fall under; it could be a person who you do not necessarily fall for in a romantic sense, but you may fall under their spell, and they could manipulate you for either financial gain, as an empath who wants to almost feed off your energy or for information and so be careful of what seems like a chance encounter and remain sceptical of new friends. Be careful of people who are too needy or too helpful and ask yourself what is their true agenda and if perhaps they have deeper issues which you may or may not want to get drawn into.

It can be a confusing and frustrating time when dealing with big companies or indeed the health service, and so remember names and dates and keep in regular contact to make sure your file is not misplaced or shoved to the bottom of the queue. If in doubt, assume you have been forgotten or sidelined and keep pushing for what you need. There can be delays regarding housing or social benefits, and you need to be aware of any innocuous changes that could actually affect you more than you think (positively or negatively).

HEALTH

Health matters often need a leap of faith this month, and Aries have to get over accepting a certain inevitability – nothing in medicine is certain, and you must explore options and never believe in absolutes. With so much information out there, we have never been as empowered regarding our health.

Fear and deep-seated anxieties, especially those which have connection to specific events in the past need to be revisited – in fact, even a recurring dream right now could be a prompt to explore something more deeply. Past life regression therapy is worth exploring as even something like sleep pattern problems, nightmares, night terrors, and anxiety can have their roots in a past life experience.

LOVE

While this month may not be so good for love, if you are expecting a forecast of mild, unchangeable weather which is not too hot or cold and pretty samey, it is very good for those who enjoy their love life weather unpredictable, dramatic, and even thundery.

Right now, Aries have a window or opportunity to make positive changes in their relationships, but you need to ask, "Who for or why am I making these changes." The universal energies will flow for you if you make the changes in good faith in a hope to better the relationship for the both of you or for the family in general; more selfish desires will be temporarily successful, but not so much in the longer term.

It is also important for you and your partner to take control over your own destiny as a couple – you need to detach from parents who seek to dictate outcomes and add pressure with no support or parents who seek to control via dogma or guilt. Make sure that your decisions are 100% your own conception and for your own future.

This is great time to invigorate relationships with new longer terms goals that can focus you and keep you on target with savings and budgets – it can be easier to work together when you have a common vision and purpose and that purpose can be concrete, i.e. holiday or home improvements or also philosophical, i.e. more time spent together as a family or educational goals for your children. Couples who can agree on what the future looks like will find some common ground no matter what the short terms issues are. The smaller matters are easily overcome for couples who are destined to be together; if you cannot see beyond tricky day to day issues right now, you may not really be all that suited in the long run.

CAREER

This is a very good month for business, money, and management decisions – Aries are both ingenious and also adaptable and innovative in the way you handle resources and use money. You can make improvements in current plans quickly, adapting to changes and seizing opportunities as you are flexible in your thinking and more willing to embrace new technology and methods.

This is a very good month for those who work in the gig economy on zero hours contracts or in the informal sector or those who perform a few different jobs as there is lots of work to choose from, and you can have some profitable opportunities that come at short notice. If you are already bogged down in work and highly committed to a schedule, you may not be able to take up many of the work-related options which come up. This month is ideal for those who are looking for a job, looking for a part time income or a second income stream. It is important to take chances and try even the long shots, and you should be as visible to employers as possible as one thing leads to another.

This is also a very good time for those in start-ups – entrepreneurs or folks with an idea that they want to develop can have some important concrete success in planning and some encouragement from mentors or people in your field. Peers are often important regarding opening your eyes to new possibilities in your field, and so any convention or meet up with like-minded professionals or workers in your line of work are worthwhile attending.

Between the 9th and 24th of September are ideal for promoting goods, foreign investment, trade arrangements to do with import and export, publishing, and also teaching. A good time to distribute literature, especially if related to personal development, spiritual awareness, social issues, and also sexual issues and gender. You have a wider audience and more influence this month to get your message across, and remember this is a good year to pass on the lessons you have learned and survival stories.

Money affairs can fluctuate, but that means there is as much chance for gain as well as loss – play your cards right.

LIFE

Impulsive reactions and also initial reactions to other people can be very strong, and while Aries usually have a keen radar, this month your first reaction may not always be accurate and so keep an open mind. Often your reactions to others are strongly linked to your own subconscious, and things that they do or what they say may trigger memories and emotions in you which have more to do with your past and who you are than who they are. Aries may have bad reactions to people who are somewhat like you used to be, perhaps you see something of you in them, something which you no longer respect about yourself as you have grown up and want to dissociate with that phase. Remember that part of this year is passing on wisdom, and you may have attracted this person so that you can teach them a valuable lesson whether they are or are not receptive.

Working with men either in relationships or at work is easier and simpler this month rather than with women. You are quite emotionally volatile, and you tend to project that inner turmoil onto women and also mother figures which are what obscures understanding and makes your interaction with women more complicated where things are often taken the wrong way or where comments and criticism come out more harshly that you expected.

HEALTH

It is best to avoid alcohol this month as it can make you volatile, and while the initial effect is to make you gregarious and fun loving, things can turn on a dime becoming more maudlin or even angry. Ulcers can flare up and so avoid raw onions, tomatoes, pineapples, fried food, and citrus fruits. Dairy is best avoided unless low fat; try hemp milk or almond milk. Avoid gluten, but do try millet, quinoa, and rice.

Anger and inner tension must be constructively dealt with. You may have to bite your lip especially to do with domestic and family matters, and that build-up of anger can create indigestion, wind, and a flare up of IBS. Physical activity generally helps you deal with any frustrations, but mental games or stimulating discussions can also be a good release as they take your mind away from matters more personal.

LOVE

Venus retrograde in Scorpio may give you the sense that something has been lost or has slipped away – indeed, you may begin to think about things that used to make you happy in the relationship and wonder why you no longer do them: what stopped you? Did life just get too busy? Did you become semi-satisfied and stop working hard at the relationships? This month is a time to stop being passive and become more active in the relationship no matter how long you have been together. It is important to look at how life transitions, usually babies, but possibly bereavement or job changes, even financial stress have impacted on your sex life. Sex life is an integral part of togetherness which you never get too old for, and it is never a bad time to reassess what is wrong and how to regenerate some spark. Marriage counselling is a very powerful tool in relationships for Aries this year as many problems have psychological roots, even though you may be convinced that it is all about physical issues or just general pressure of life.

This is an excellent time to look at the link between sexual performance and health as sex drive or lack of it could be linked to health issues which can be addressed – so this month is ideal for breaking down taboos and hang-ups you are having regarding your sex life.

Promises kept and loyalty are essential elements in relationships, and so make sure you have your partner's back – sometimes your partner just wants to know you are behind them and does not want an analysis of the situation. Throwing your pennies' worth in can make you appear critical and unsupportive, and so just support without the commentary.

Some of the old mixed in with the new can bring the fun back, and so try what used to work and see if it brings back the spark. In some cases, you have matured and grown out of the old things, but you can always discover new things together which makes your togetherness an adventure and a growth experience.

Never forget the small things that are so sweet and so precious in your relationship, while you hanker after the bigger goals we are all encouraged to long for today.

Finding you and your partner's unique rhythm in sexual relationships is something that cannot be expected to just happen, and you have to use a combination of oral and penetrative with masturbation and even some porn (if that is your thing) to bridge gaps between you in desire. It is also very important to compliment your partner sexually – not glib, vague or clichéd comments, make your compliments very specific and thoughtful.

CAREER

Between the new moon on 8 October and full moon on the 24th are good times for important events connected to new starts and initiations. Not such a good time for new IT systems or changing your business operating software as there are too many unknowns. Power games and vested interests can also make it hard for you to take control and implement changes that you feel would benefit your workplace. Colleagues can be erratic and also unpredictable – they may let you down last minute, and so make sure when you set targets you have back up regarding being able to call on others last minute to pick up the pieces if someone does wimp out.

This is a time when details and fine print to do with money cannot be ignored, and you cannot have mind gaps where there are things you just do not understand and are just hoping will never come up.

Ideas and plans need to be very flexible right now and must take account of any shocks or external events out of your control which may come to pass – contingency plans and extra time built in are very important.

Artistic projects like writing or entertaining are that much more successful and gripping when you pick up on current social events and weave that thread through your work. Timing and sensing the right time creatively is vital – you cannot just jump in, you must test the water and get the feel of your competition and the market.

Market research is both important and successful right now; the key is knowing what you are looking for in the first place and devising the right questions to make sure you get appropriate information.

LIFE

Your willingness regarding expanding your consciousness and the scope of your interactions with others is high. You want to grow, and you want to do that by joining hands, bridging gaps, and thinking philosophically. Aries are magnanimous and open-hearted, and this draws more positive experiences to you and helps you attract the sort of people who can introduce you to or lead you into new adventures both physical and intellectual.

Relations with others are really good this month, perhaps because you are bringing the best out of them via the positive vibe you are projecting.

People who come into your life right now will have a positive impact, they will help you to understand more about opportunities and how to exploit them.

This is quite an idealistic time, but not necessarily a time when you are unproductive because you are wearing rose coloured glasses. You are very proactive in sowing seeds and setting some new challenge up to tackle – these challenges are often not material, but more in terms of testing your character and being more involved in life away from your immediate circle of friends, colleagues, and relatives.

Long distance travel to a place you have never been before is highly possible at this time. Even if you do not travel a great distance from where you live, you will find yourself in another world, possibly one you never knew much about before.

Between the 7th and 23rd are the best times for action and initiation especially regarding romance and new dates, negotiations, and business deals, trade, innovation, and sports.

Aries are very skilful with their hands and are often excellent at creative work involving dexterity i.e. hairdressing, clothes making, crafts and even surgery – this month all these activities are enhanced.

HEALTH

Karma operates in your favour bringing good turns your way. However, giving is better than receiving, and Aries gain from the process of being generous.

Using mental imagery to focus healing white light on your own body or that of a friend or family member is very effective. Positive thoughts have added potency during this phase as you are naturally able to generate them without having to suppress a creeping critical or cynical vibe.

A very uncynical attitude and a lack of stubborn adherence to dogma or to outworn ideas mean that your body will respond favourably and be able to heal itself.

Forgiveness at this time is also both healing and transformative on a physical and emotional level.

Some Aries will experience insomnia during this phase of Mars entering Pisces on the 15th, especially if you have not allowed yourself an opportunity to recoup and if you do not listen to the subtle signals your body gives you.

LOVE

Nothing can be taken for granted in love, and even the good parts of the relationship need work and attention. If you are having to be in cruise mode regarding love, and that goes for marriages and also dating, your partner may suddenly kick up his/her heels and begin demanding more affection and also your focus.

Aries can be a little lazy about the tender aspects of lovemaking – you could be less willing to engage in extended foreplay or romantic conversation, and yet these are exactly the areas of sex and intimacy you need to improve on this month.

You also need to be more diplomatic and less driven when pushing for the things you want – if you find selfish needs hard to restrain, then maybe you are just not as into this person as you should be if you are dating or supposedly in love. Often selfishness tells a story about how close to the sell by date of the relationship you are. If married, you should take a long hard look at where you are and ask yourself if you really should be doing more and putting certain other aims on the shelf for the sake of a marriage.

No relationship can offer everything that Aries needs right now as you are combustible, insatiable, and full of sexual energy so there is no need to get doubts about a relationship that is not 100% fulfilling as that would be impossible (unless your partner is Aries too or Scorpio). What you do need to do is reach compromises so that your life can expand in other areas especially creatively to fill that gap.

Relationships that rely heavily on habit regarding the way you react to each other, must have a shakeup. Just because you have always done it one way is probably a good reason to scrap that as a routine and get your imagination working on developing some more thrilling habits.

Be honest about your desires, listen to your partner, and get rid of what doesn't work – who knows, if you actually talked more about sex, you may find out that certain things would be on both of your list to BIN.

Mid-month is the most telling time for relationships with Mercury going direct and Venus going retrograde, but with Mars entering Pisces, I am pretty sure Arians will have the charisma, panache, and wild imagination to envisage a more exciting outcome for the evenings.

CAREER

This month Aries who have just begun to study at university or who are mature students looking to take a degree course or do higher learning get a massive boost. Study you undertake right now is not just about what you learn in technical or academic sense it is about discovering more about you, your place in the world, widening your expectations of yourself and learning more about how to work with others.

Aries are powerful motivators this month – as team leader you can gee others up and inspire them towards a goal. Thanks to your leadership, the sum of the parts is more than the whole due to the ethos of enthusiasm and belief.

This is a very effective time for Arians who write, publish, or sell ideas – in fact, you may be in the right place at the right time to capitalise on an emerging trend or mass need of the public. Look for what others want, and provide the answers.

Mercury retrograde from the 16th of the month does not mean that plans and operations go into reverse; however, it does mean that you must sure up the details, re-edit, and fine tune making sure you foresee glitches. This is not a time to 'rush to press' as accuracy means more than timeliness, and so get it right rather than getting it out first.

You may realise that you have overlooked some smaller yet significant details as you were so carried away with the goal and the broader ideal – even the fanciest, diamond encrusted watch needs the cogs and wheels to click perfectly together or what use is it?

This is also a time to reflect upon your goals. Often past actions catch up with you – and this need not be a bad thing if it forces you to clarify in your own mind what you are trying to achieve.

Energy must also be channelled into the most private matters of your life, those which matter to you but which you do not share with others.

LIFE

Aries are able to hone in on problem areas in their work life, health, and also regarding relationships (both romantic or family) and direct a laser beam of energy onto that problem in order to get to grips with it and shrink it down to size. Your determination to deal with things of importance is high, and you will come out on top allowing nothing to get the better of you. You can be quite intimidating, and whoever wants to take you on is in for a battle as you are not for turning.

Before rolling your sleeves up, you do have to be honest with yourself about priorities as if you spread your energies over a wider spectrum hoping to lick a range of issue into shape, you could be in for frustrations and mismanagement of time.

Jupiter trine your return Mercury encourages you to take the plunge in all communications – do not wait for the call to come, chase it up and follow things up. Making chance off the cuff phone calls may help you to create an opportunity or make a great impression, showing your enthusiasm.

With the new moon on the 6th and Mercury going direct on the 8th, you are all set to go for the Christmas season; work and admin goals should be achieved, logistically things flow, the weather should play ball, any correspondence should be finished in time, study and teaching related work are on target and financial matters should be hitchless. You must be careful not to overcommit as you could be vulnerable to seasonal flu if you get run down. While most affairs of life are successful in the run up to Christmas, you must not try to be all things to all people or get caught up in the folly of others. Ferry trips should be avoided.

HEALTH

Bone health issues may come to light, and there are a number of things you need to think about. Are you getting enough calcium? Often you either have a shortage of calcium or a shortage of iron, as these two minerals cannot be absorbed together and supplements that have both in are pretty well useless as they inhibit each other's absorption. If you think you are calcium deficient, find a quality supplement.

At this time of year in the Northern Hemisphere, we do not get much quality light, and you may have a shortage of vitamin D which can also affect bones as well as your immune system, and so make sure you get some vitamin D3.

Arthritis may flare up, and so eat foods with low acidity or even drink alkaline water (available online). To help arthritis and any inflammation issues (associated with injury), limit dairy, processed and all white foods (i.e. white sugar, flour, bread, pasta). Turmeric taken with honey aids swelling and joint pain.

Jupiter brings success in terms of improving health where you are both positive and proactive – you do not have to be very strict, but you do have to have a committed attitude.

LOVE

The office party is definitely an event which requires a red warning light – sudden romances with colleagues are to be avoided. I know it is the season to be jolly, but love and alcohol are not good bedfellows – do not don the beer goggles and get led into a romance that is ill conceived.

Marriages fare very well in December, much better than first time dates and forays into the clubbing and partying world. The planets suggest that new people you meet, especially in the party environment could be false or superficial and anything but what they seem, and so you really should wait until January comes before you get excited, to see how it all looks in the sober light of the new year.

Marriages are harmonious, and there is more understanding – men are more in tune with their female side, and women with their more masculine side, and that brings balance and greater cooperation on family matters and generally. A greater degree of relaxation aids sexual encounters. Aries are romantically inspired, and a positive frame of mind about relationships regarding the physical and emotional side does wonders now. Familiarity and comfort are dominant motivators for you during this month. It's a good time to mend relationship problems and to surround yourself with people.

If single, your romantic side will have added colour and diversity. You're romantic, for sure, but a little inclined to self-deception by seeing an image you create in your head rather than reality. Being "in love with love" is quite possible now. You may find yourself falling for a person who is elusive, or are they just unattainable? Drama in romance can be lovely, but do you really need the confusion?

CAREER

Your greatest strength this month is knowing your limitations and also how to work around them. Often you can take a weakness, work on it, and realise that you are actually quite good at it and were just going about it the wrong way – things in that regard can suddenly click for you.

This December represents a period of quite satisfying culmination where you feel the efforts of the year have paid off, and you are now in a position to take that momentum forward.

There can be increased responsibility not only via your position in the command chain but also via obligations to government bodies or other corporations.

Recognition and news of a pay rise or improvement in job situations can come to you this month.

Working within systems is the best way to get the most done, and so appeasement of your superiors and retraining that natural hot-headed approach will see you make faster progress with better results. Not a time to cut off your nose to spite your face; pick your battles, and do not start fighting causes that are not pivotal to your core aims.

A positive month for buying and selling – if you trade, this should be a strong Christmas season with robust sales of products especially products that are imported, connected to communications, or sporting goods.

Work in social care and the medical fields are busy but inspiring, and a comradery can help you cope with increased workload.

While Saturn brings the need for commitment and hard work with strong management skills, Jupiter brings enjoyment, progress, and zest to keep you and others going.

It is a very strong yet serious minded end to the year, and Aries are keen to go out, perhaps not with a bang, but with plenty of bang for their buck – yes, results count, and you are nailing this 'end of the year' making sure you hit targets and impress your clients, colleagues, and superiors.

THANK YOU VERY MUCH FOR BUYING THIS BOOK AND SUPPORTING MY WORK – GOD BLESS AND HAVE A GREAT 2018 AND 2019.